DK ELT Graded Readers

ELEMENTARY A

TWISTERS

Written by Mike Potter

Series Editor Susan Holden

A Dorling Kindersley Book

Rob was in his farmyard in Texas. It was a quiet and peaceful spring day and he wanted to take his dog, Barney, for a walk. But he couldn't find him anywhere. Finally, he saw where Barney was. He was underneath the tractor. Barney looked frightened and didn't move when Rob called him. Rob couldn't understand what was the matter with his dog. He didn't usually behave in this strange way. Normally, Barney loved his walks. He always ran up to Rob and wagged his tail happily. But today, Barney didn't want to move at all. "Perhaps he's ill," Rob thought.

To the reader:

Welcome to the DK ELT Graded Readers! These readers are different. They explore aspects of the world around us: its history, geography, science ... and a lot of other things. And they show the different ways in which people live now, and lived in the past.

These DK ELT Graded Readers give you material for reading for information, and reading for pleasure. You are using your English to do something real. The illustrations will help you understand the text, and also help bring the Reader to life. There is a glossary to help you understand the special words for this topic. Listen to the cassette or CD as well, and you can really enter the world of the Olympic Games, the *Titanic*, or the Trojan War ... and a lot more. Choose the topics that interest you, improve your English, and learn something ... all at the same time.
Enjoy the series!

To the teacher:

This series provides varied reading practice at five levels of language difficulty, from elementary to FCE level:
BEGINNER
ELEMENTARY A
ELEMENTARY B
INTERMEDIATE
UPPER INTERMEDIATE
The language syllabus has been designed to suit the factual nature of the series, and includes a wider vocabulary range than is usual with ELT readers: language linked with the specific theme of each book is included and glossed. The language scheme, and ideas for exploiting the material (including the recorded material) both in and out of class are contained in the Teacher's Resource Book.
We hope you and your students enjoy using this series.

Dorling DK Kindersley

LONDON, NEW YORK, SYDNEY, DELHI,
PARIS, MUNICH & JOHANNESBURG

Originally published as Dorling Kindersley
Reader *Twisters!* in 2000 and adapted as an
ELT Graded Reader for
Dorling Kindersley by

studio cactus ©

13 SOUTHGATE STREET   WINCHESTER   HAMPSHIRE   SO23 9DZ

Published in Great Britain by
Dorling Kindersley Limited
9 Henrietta Street, London WC2E 8PS

2 4 6 8 10 9 7 5 3 1

Copyright © 2000
Dorling Kindersley Limited, London

A CIP catalogue record for this book is
available from the British Library.

ISBN 0-7513-2937-1

Colour reproduction by Colourscan, Singapore
Printed and bound in China by
L. Rex Printing Co., Ltd
Text film output by Chimera.trt, UK

The publisher would like to thank the following
for their kind permission to reproduce their photographs:
c=centre; t=top; b=below; l=left; r=right

National Geographic Image Collection: Chris Johns 26–27b; NOAA
Photo Library/NOAA Central Library (www.photolib.noaa.gov/):
28t, 30; Planet Earth Pictures: Alex Benwell 15br, Paolo Fancialli 6tr,
Robert Harding Picture Library: 10, Sheila Beougher 18bl,
Warren Faidley/Agliolo 1br, Warren Faidley/Int'l Stock 16–17, 18tr, Jeff
Greenberg 22tr; Tony Stone Images: 21tr, Christoph Burki 5tr, Jerry
Kobalenko 4, 5, Alan R Mollet 19b, Camille Tokerud 15cr; Topham
Picturepoint: 25br, J. McTyre 24.
Jacket: Robert Harding Picture Library

See our complete catalogue at

www.dk.com

Suddenly, the sky became black. First, heavy rain
began to fall. Huge hailstones – the size of golf balls
– started to pour down from the sky. Then came the
thunder and lightning. The noise was terrible.

Rob crawled under the tractor to escape the
lightning and the hail. He stroked his frightened dog
and calmed him. The rain, hail and thunder
suddenly stopped. Everything became strangely still
and quiet. Rob looked at Barney. Now he
understood why his dog didn't want to go for a walk
that morning. He crawled out from underneath the
tractor. His clothes were covered with mud. He
called Barney. The dog looked calmer now, but he
still did not want to leave the safety of the tractor.

Rob walked over to the fence and looked out over the countryside. He didn't like what he saw. Near the hills, in the distance, there were huge black clouds. They began to turn like a child's spinning top. Then they started to bubble – just like milk boiling in a saucepan. The wind began to blow again. Its strong gusts reached the farm and blew the straw in the farmyard high into the sky. Next, a dark finger of cloud reached down from the centre of the black clouds and started to move towards the ground. Rob knew what was going to happen. This cloud was a twister. Perhaps it was going to move towards his farm!

He looked on helplessly, but there was nothing that he could do. The cloud became blacker and blacker. Now it had a life of its own. It began to turn faster and faster. For a time, the finger of cloud moved from side to side, backwards and forwards, like the trunk of a gigantic elephant looking for food on the dry earth. Finally, the twister touched the ground. Mud and grass swirled up like smoke from a bonfire. But this was only the beginning.

The twister began to move forwards towards Rob's farm. It gathered speed quickly as it skipped and bounced across the fields. It grew bigger, faster and dirtier every minute, and sucked up all the mud, bushes and fences – everything that it met.

Waterspouts
Waterspouts are twisters that happen out at sea. They whisk up water. The tallest waterspouts can be 1.6 kilometres high.

Rob watched the twister in horror. It reached his neighbour's farm. It was very fierce now. It ripped up bushes and trees – and even a tractor and a farm truck. It lifted them high into the air and spun them around. It even destroyed farm buildings as it swept past them. The tractor and farm truck shot through the air like a rocket and fell to the earth with a loud crash. At least they didn't fall on Rob's farm.

For a moment, the twister changed direction and moved back towards the hills. Rob sighed with relief – but not for long. It swiftly changed direction again. And this time, it started to move straight towards him. He had to act quickly. There was little time left!

The twister rushed through his fields and soon reached the farm. Rob heard a noise like a waterfall crashing down a mountain. He looked behind him and could not believe his eyes. There was a loud BANG! – like the noise of an exploding bomb. The barn, where he kept his hay and straw, collapsed as the hungry twister sucked up the roof, windows and everything inside it.

Rob had to run for his life. Luckily, he saw Barney and grabbed him. He ran towards the cellar of his house. But the wind was strong and tried to suck him inside the twister. His ears hurt and it was difficult to breathe. That was because the air pressure inside a twister is very low. It makes people's ears ache, and causes buildings to explode. Rob reached his house just in time!

He rushed into the cellar and managed to lock its heavy door. The twister struck the house. The front door flew off with a loud CRASH! Then there was a SMASH and all the house windows blew in. The noise and fury of the wind seemed to last forever, but after only two minutes, all was silent again.

Rob came up from the cellar. He looked at the damage. His furniture lay all over the floor, in pieces. There were bits of wood, glass and broken cups and dishes everywhere. Amazingly, there were still one or two pictures on the wall. But most of the doors were not there anymore, and there was no glass in the windows.

Rob felt lucky to be alive.

Some friends, who lived nearby, came to help
Rob to clean up his house. They were lucky.
Their house did not lie in the twister's path,
and they and all their belongings were safe.

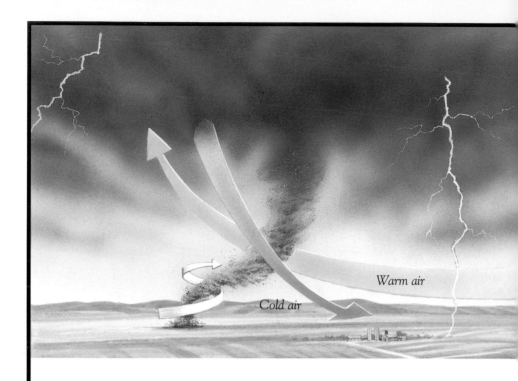

Warm air

Cold air

Twisters can begin to form when warm air meets cold air. A dark cloud forms and starts to suck up the warm air from the ground. Soon there is a swirling column of cloud that reaches down from the dark cloud in search of more warm air. This column is a funnel cloud. It spins at great speed and sucks up everything in its path. The inside of a twister contains some of the most dangerous and deadly winds in the world.

Great streaks of lightning shoot down from the dark cloud as the twister builds up its strength. Terrifying claps of thunder echo across the countryside when the lightning strikes the ground.

Twisters are dangerous and unpredictable. No one can tell exactly what they are, or where they are going to move next. They can lift up a large truck and smash it to pieces, but they often leave small objects, like pictures or books, undamaged.

Sometimes some very unexpected and strange things happen when twisters pass by. They can even be surprisingly gentle! One twister picked up a baby when he was asleep and set him down safely 90 metres away. The baby didn't even wake up. He didn't know about the twister. His parents couldn't believe their eyes, or their good luck.

Strange showers

When twisters drop the things that they pick up, strange things can happen. A twister in England once caused a shower of frogs to fall to the ground.

There are a lot of strange stories about twisters. Some of them are difficult to believe, but they are true!

For example, a twister once blew away a man's birth certificate. The twister sucked it up and carried it for 80 kilometres and then dropped it in a friend's garden. Can you imagine the man's surprise when his friend telephoned him and asked him, "Why did you send me your birth certificate?"

One twister sucked up some roses and water from a vase. It dropped them in another room, but it left the vase on the table.

Another twister opened the doors of a kitchen cupboard and sucked out a jar of pickles. It carried the jar over a very long distance and let it fall gently back to the ground. The jar did not break, and the pickles inside it were ready for someone to eat!

Twisters come in many different shapes and sizes. Some can be thin, white and wispy. In fact, they don't look dangerous at all. But when most people think of twisters, they imagine a thick, black cloud, with a long, tight funnel that swirls in all directions.

But did you know that twisters come in all sorts of colours, as well as shapes and sizes?

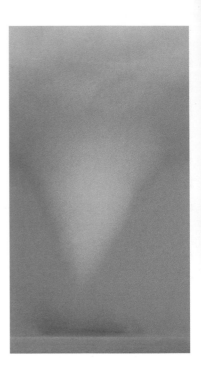

Twisters can even be red. Sometimes a twister sucks up red earth, and it becomes the same colour as the earth. In the same way, when a twister travels over a muddy field, it becomes brown – and very smelly!

Twisters can grow bigger and faster as they move along. They can also change their shape. When you see some twisters, you may think that they have a loop or a knot in the middle. Others are wider at the bottom than they are at the top. Most funnel clouds look like a twisting tube, but others don't look like a funnel at all. They look more like a wide piece of cake, or a slice of pie.

Sometimes, twisters do no damage at all. They start as a small whirlwind moving across the hot, dry earth, but the weather conditions are not right and they do not develop. However, bigger twisters are very dangerous because it is impossible to know their strength or the direction they are going to take.

Lots of people know
what a twister looks like
from the outside. But not
many people know what it is
like to be inside one, or are still alive
to be able to describe their experience.

Will Kelly was a farmer who once saw
what the inside of a twister was like. He saw
and heard the twister as it approached his home.
He ran towards his underground shelter and reached
it just in time. He jumped inside and tried to close
the door, but the wind was too strong. It pulled the
door upwards towards the funnel. Somehow, Will
managed to cling on to the door, and this probably
saved his life.

However, when he looked up, he saw that he
was in the middle of the funnel. Inside the big
twister, there were lots of smaller twisters that
moved in every direction. These small twisters are
very strong and powerful and can rip through a
building and destroy it completely, like an electric
saw when it cuts through the trunk of a thick tree.

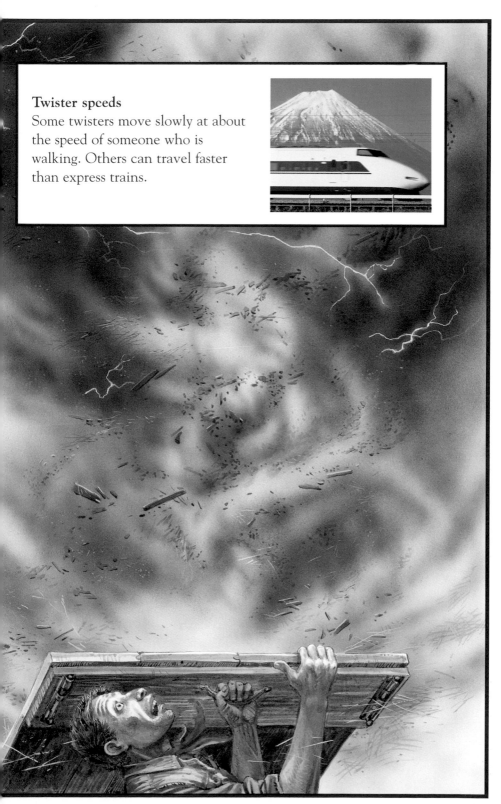

Twister speeds
Some twisters move slowly at about the speed of someone who is walking. Others can travel faster than express trains.

Home is always home
People stay in Tornado Alley because it is their home. If a tornado destroys their house, they just build it again.

People frequently call twisters "tornados". There is an area in the centre of the USA that everybody knows as Tornado Alley. It is famous all over the world because of the deadly twisters that frequently happen there.

The most dangerous time for twisters is between April and July. Every year, they kill more than 80 people in this part of the United States.

At this time of year, the weather in the north is still cold. But in the south, it is beginning to become warmer. The cold air comes down from the north and meets the warmer air from the south – right over Tornado Alley.

TORNADO ALLEY

People grade twisters on a scale of 0–5. This scale is known as the Fujita Scale. F0 twisters are the weakest and F5 ones are the strongest and most dangerous.

An F0 damages chimneys on the roofs of houses.

An F1 breaks telephone poles.

An F2 tears the roofs off houses and small buildings.

An F3 turns over railway trains.

An F4 destroys strong, solid houses.

An F5 destroys nearly everything in its path. In 1999, an F5 ripped through Oklahoma City in the State of Oklahoma. Oklahoma is in the heart of Tornado Alley. The powerful twister killed 45 people. It lifted off the roofs and sides of many houses and completely destroyed many more buildings. A lot of people lost their cars, kitchen equipment and other precious possessions as the twister cut its path through their homes.

The worst twister
In 1925, one twister in Tornado Alley destroyed four towns in only four hours. It killed 689 people.

Twisters often happen in Tornado Alley. The people who live there have to protect themselves during the tornado season. Most of them build strong underground shelters outside their homes and climb into them when they hear that a tornado is approaching.

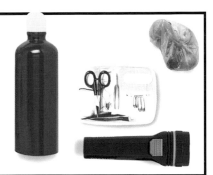

Emergency supplies
People keep emergency supplies in their shelters – food, drink, torches and a first-aid kit.

In Texas, fibreglass shelters are very popular. People dig a large hole in their back garden and bury the shelter there.

Some people do not have shelters outside their home or in their garden. When a tornado comes, they have to hide in a cellar or small room in the middle of their house.

The Malones are standing next to their fibreglass shelter, which they are soon going to bury in their garden.

Gary England is a TV weather reporter in Oklahoma City. During the tornado season, when they can expect lots of twisters, Gary and his team follow the path of all the tornados in the area. Sometimes they stay in the TV studio for more than 30 hours.

Scientists tell Gary what the weather is going to be like. He and his team then pass on the information to the TV viewers. The scientists use a computer that helps them to find where a twister is going to develop. Then, the computer makes a picture that shows a twister's position, the direction that it is taking and its speed.

The team watch the computer all the time; they have to be very careful to observe and write down any changes of direction. Gary's work has saved many lives. He has to make sure that his viewers always have accurate information about the twister's course and its strength. They need plenty of time to take shelter.

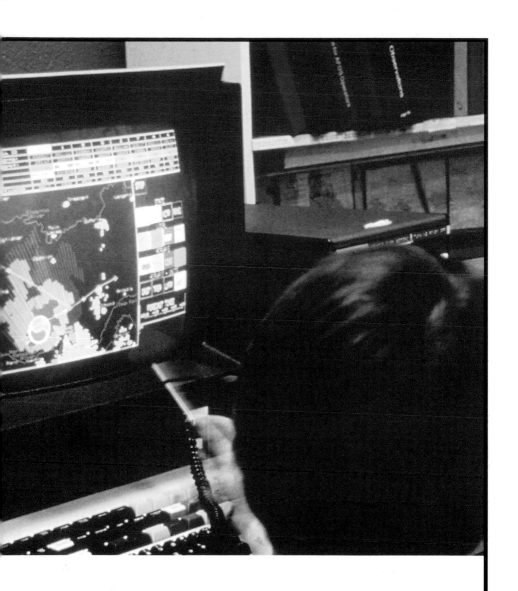

Weather information from space
Spacecraft called satellites orbit
around Earth. Some send
information about the weather
to scientists on Earth.

The scientists tell Gary what they think is going to happen. But they never know what is really happening, or the direction that a twister is following. That is the job of the storm trackers, who are out on the roads in their vehicles during the tornado season, looking out for new twisters.

Many trackers drive large trucks with a lot of modern equipment, like satellite dishes, on them. These people risk their lives to find and follow twisters. Sometimes, a twister unexpectedly changes its course and heads in their direction. When this happens, it is not the storm trackers who are tracking the twister – it is the twister that is tracking them!

The trackers are often more accurate than the computer. They can tell Gary everything he wants to know about a twister – where it is and where it is going. They can even tell him when a twister is going to form before it appears on any computer screen.

In the days before trackers and TV existed, people did not have any information about dangerous twisters near their homes. Many of them had only a little time or no time at all to prepare for the disaster that was going to strike. Some did not know about the twister until it was too late.

Thanks to modern technology and the work of the trackers and scientists, most people now have time to prepare themselves.

A storm tracker's modern truck.

Glossary

to approach
To come near.

birth certificate
The official document that shows your name, parents and date of birth.

bonfire
A fire that people light outdoors to burn rubbish or to keep warm.

cellar
A room underneath the ground floor of a house, where people can store things.

to collapse
To fall down.

to crawl
To move on your hands and knees, like a baby.

deadly
Something very dangerous that can cause death.

ear-splitting
A very loud and sudden noise that can make a person deaf for a short time.

experience
An event that happens to you.

fence
A wooden "wall" around a garden or field.

fibreglass
A strong but light material that people use in the construction of houses and many industrial products.

funnel cloud
The swirling column of cloud that forms when a twister sucks up warm air.

to grade
To put things in order of size, strength or measurement.

gust
A strong burst of wind.

hailstones
Rain that forms into ice before it reaches the ground.

helplessly
You are helpless when you can do nothing to stop something from happening.

jar
A glass container, e.g. for jam and preserved fruit and vegetables.

muddy
When it rains a lot, the ground in the country or in the garden becomes muddy.

orbit
The circular path that an object follows in space, e.g. the Earth's orbit.